Come Shop with Me

Discovering Microservices One Store at a Time

Come Shop with Me

Discovering Microservices One Store at a Time

ATIF A.EDEN

ISBN 9798336764147

In loving memory of my brother Bassit, whose life exemplified success, strength, and dignity. You were a guiding light, showing me how to navigate life's challenges with grace and determination. May the lord envelop your soul in eternal mercy.

Brief contents

Contents

Preface

In recent years, the landscape of software development has shifted dramatically. As applications have become more complex, the demand for flexible, scalable, and maintainable architectures has increased. Enter microservices, a novel concept that divides monolithic programs into smaller, independently deployable services. While this notion may appear difficult, my goal with this book is to make it understandable and relevant to everyone, regardless of technical background.

"Come Shop with Me: Discovering Microservices One Store at a Time." employs the well-known shopping mall analogy to highlight the complexities of microservices architecture. Microservices enable developers to create modular and adaptive applications, much like a mall is a thriving ecosystem packed with varied retailers, each fulfilling a specific purpose.

This book will walk you through the numerous architectural styles, cloud services, and design patterns that support microservices, making the complex world of software development feels more like a leisurely shopping experience. Throughout this journey, you will encounter a variety of subjects, including monolithic and client-server architectures, service-oriented architecture, and the fundamentals of microservices. We will look at key aspects like scalability, service discovery, and communication patterns, all within the framework of our shopping mall analogy. Each chapter is aimed to deliver insights and practical information, so you may learn the principles of microservices while having fun.

Whether you are a seasoned developer who has never worked with microservice architecture, an aspiring software engineer, or simply inquisitive about modern technology, this book is for you. I hope that at the end of our adventure, you will not only comprehend microservices but also appreciate their elegance and power in software development.

Thank you for accompanying me on this adventure. Let us enter the mall and explore the world of microservices together!

Acknowledgements

I want to sincerely thank my parents for being the cornerstone of my path with their constant support and encouragement. I would especially like to thank my wife and daughter for their love, support, and tolerance over the many hours I spent creating this book. Your confidence in me has always given me motivation.

In addition, I want to pay tribute to my brother, whose memory inspires me every day. I hope he finds peace.

Finally, I would want to acknowledge the difficult economic times we have been through, which have, rather surprisingly, given me the chance to concentrate on and finish this book. These experiences have taught me the value of perseverance and the necessity of following our passions during challenging times.

About the author

Atif A. Eden The mastermind behind an innovative writing style that simplifies complex technical concepts. He is a visionary Java programmer who distills complex technical concepts into understandable knowledge. With over a decade of experience developing groundbreaking software solutions, Atif has impacted clients in North Africa, France, Belgium, Canada, and the United States.

His expertise in technologies such as the Spring Framework and Amazon Web Services (AWS) is unparalleled. Atif's innovative writing style simplifies complex technical concepts using analogies and real-world examples, making them understandable to a wide range of readers.

Atif, an accomplished author, has written several essential books for developers that demystify software development and architecture through simple jargon and relatable insights. Atif can be reached via atifaeden@gmail.com.

The Giraffe symbol on the cover

Why a giraffe on the cover of a book about microservices? one may think. Its distinct skin pattern holds the answer. Similar to how apps are divided into manageable modules by microservices architecture, a giraffe's coat is made up of several patches. Every patch operates alone and as a cohesive unit, much like a microservice. Think of each spot as an individual API:

- **Unique/Related:** Each spot is unique but part of a larger system.

- **Modular Design**: Each location has a distinct function within the larger framework.

- **Scalability**: A giraffe's pattern widens with growth, just as microservices do on their own.

- **Adaptability**: Modular versatility is demonstrated by the slightly varying patterns on each giraffe.

By representing microservices as giraffe spots, we can better grasp how different parts come together to form a dependable, adaptable, and scalable system. Keep in mind that giraffes are nature's examples of microservices architecture the next time you see one!

Introduction

Welcome to "Come Shop with Me: Discovering Microservices One Store at a Time." Imagine walking into a crowded retail mall, each store, kiosk, and service representing a different component of modern software design. This book takes you on a unique tour into the world of microservices, utilizing the familiar setting of a shopping mall to explain complicated technology principles.

As we go around our metaphorical mall, we'll see a variety of architectural types, from all-in-one department stores (monolithic architecture) to specialized boutiques (microservices). We'll explore the mall's infrastructure, looking at how various services are delivered, from the foundation (IaaS) to the ready-to-use stores (SaaS).

Our voyage will take us through the mall's revolutionary features, including its smart directory (service discovery) and efficient layout (loose coupling). We'll study how the mall responds to peak seasons (scalability) and unexpected closures (circuit breakers and fallbacks).

Communication is essential in any business, and we'll look at both synchronous (real-time interactions) and asynchronous (delayed answers) approaches. We'll also go behind the scenes to see how each store manages its inventory (using microservice databases).

No mall is complete without good administration, therefore we'll look into logging, monitoring, and alert systems. Finally, we'll look at the mall's security procedures, including how OAuth 2 protects our microservices.

By the end of this tour, you'll have a thorough grasp of microservices architecture, all taught in the familiar and relatable context of a shopping mall. So, grab your shopping cart and let's dive into the thrilling world of microservices!

Architectural Odyssey

Prior to discussing the microservices architecture and its characteristics. let's take a look at the timeline history of the main different architectural styles. One of the earliest architectural styles used in software development was the monolithic architecture. But what does a monolith mean after all?

1. Monolithic architecture

A monolith is a geological feature consisting of a single massive stone or rock, such as some mountains. Erosion usually exposes the geological formations, which are often made of very hard and solid

3

igneous or metamorphic rock. Some monoliths are volcanic plugs,

solidified lava filling the vent of an extinct volcano.

Wikipedia

In the IT field, a monolith architecture is where the entire application is built as a single, self-contained unit. This way of design created significant maintenance and scaling challenges as the monolithic application grew in complexity.

$$***$$

2. Client-server architecture

The optimal answer to these challenges was the

implementation of the 2-tier (a.k.a client-server) architecture, that aims to separate the application into a client and a server, allowing for better scalability and separation of concerns.

However, it turned out that it was limited in terms of scalability and maintainability, especially for more complex applications.

3. Three-tier architecture

So to make the 2-tier architecture
more optimal, the 3-tier architecture
emerged and promised to introduce an
intermediate application layer, allowing

further separation of concerns and scalability enhancement, it

consists, basically, of a single presentation tier, logic tier, and data

tier. Unfortunately, once put to the test, it was found that this

architecture is also limited in its ability to adapt to changing

requirements and technologies under certain circumstances.

✳✳✳

4. Service-oriented architecture

The next major shift was the introduction of the SOA (Service-

Oriented Architecture), which aimed to improve flexibility and

reusability by structuring applications as a collection of services. It

mainly aimed to improve flexibility, reusability, and

interoperability compared to the previous architecture.

However, this architecture still involves some level of centralized governance and orchestration and emphasizes large, coarse-grained services representing broader functional components.

To understand this better, let's consider this use case: A banking application with several services, where the 1st service is a Wealth manager that allows managing customers' Portfolios, and transactions, and checks for potential frauds. Whereas the 2nd service is the funding manager which is responsible for bank accounts and agreements management. Both services are shown below in a schematic form:

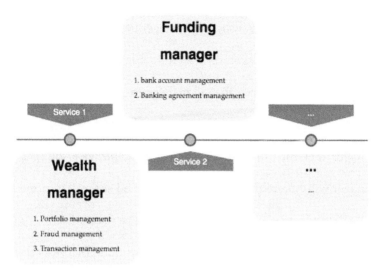

Figure 4.1: Coarse-grained services

The service 1 centralizes 3 potential fine-grained services: the first one is the portfolio manager who is responsible for building and overseeing a selection of assets like stocks, bonds, and cash that meet the customer's long-term financial goals.

The second one: the fraud manager employs real-time analyses of application data to flag discrepancies, such as inconsistent information or unusual patterns, etc..

The last one: the transaction manager processes the necessary database queries and changes in order to check their account balance, subtract the requested amount, update the bank's records and release the dispensed cash.

That being said, the transaction manager besides its core task presented above, always starts with initiating a call to the Fraud Manager Service to verify that all matters are resolved correctly. The latter, if it returns a positive response to the transaction manager, then the transaction is completed. Otherwise, the fraud manager will ensure that the parties concerned are well informed of the detected case and the transaction will be rejected.

When a new feature for one of the aforementioned services is needed, for instance, let's admit that the bank wanted to broaden the list of benefits offered to customers who hold an asset with the bank. The involved service in this example is obviously service 1, especially the portfolio management section. Once the new feature is implemented, tested, and approved to go on production, the whole service must be taken offline. Although stopping the whole service for a while is blocking, in an inappropriate way, customers who are willing to conduct standard transactions, it seems that this has an expensive cost for the bank, which risks losing not only tremendous money but also having unsatisfied customers, especially if the patches and new features are done in a high frequency!

***

5. Microservices architecture

Finally, the microservices architecture (aka N-tier architecture) evolved from SOA, emphasizing further the benefits of modularity, scalability, and independent deployment of services. In other terms, it focuses on breaking down an application into small, independent services also known as APIs: Application Programming Interfaces, responsible for specific business capabilities. which promotes a highly decentralized and autonomous approach, where each service can be developed, deployed, and scaled independently. The whole ecosystem will turn into several APIs and will look as the illustration in figure 5.1.

Each API operates independently and possesses its own

database. Thus, the portfolio manager becomes a unique independent API, as well as the Fraud and Transaction managers. This means that after making fixes or adding new features to one of them, it is only the concerned one that will be stopped when re-deployed, while the rest remain untouched.

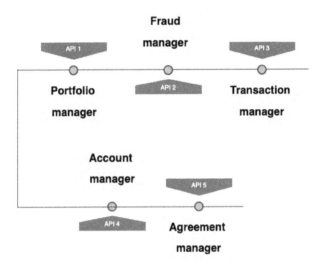

Figure 5.1: Fine-grained services

Like this, if we take back the figure 4.1, the coarse-grained service 1 will turn into three fine-grained, totally autonomous services, the service 2 will have the same destiny as well. So, with this new architecture of microservices, when the bank tries to add a new feature that consists of broadening the advantages list for their customer with assets, the involved service is going to be, of course, the portfolio service, and customers aiming to conduct new transactions will be always able to do it through the transaction manager API even though it will be communicating to the fraud API to get the next appropriate action to perform. consequently, only the portfolio customers will notice that the portfolio service has been out for a while. At the same time, unconcerned customers will always continue performing transactions without having the knowledge that another service is being updated.

Generally, we got two main types of communication between those services / APIs:

➢ **Synchronous communication**

➢ **Asynchronous communication**

In the upcoming chapters, we will go deeper into both forms of communication using an analogy to a shopping center. All you need to know right now is that services / APIs are able to communicate with each other via the HTTP protocol (synchronous communication) or events / messages (asynchronous communication). The fact that services are fine-grained in the microservices architecture allows companies to become more efficient in terms of project management, for instance, the company will place a team per API, where each team is going to have the number of the required developers according to the workload to be provided to satisfy the bank's clients.

The aforementioned microservices concepts are only a few among a big list of fundamental notions that must be incorporated into the microservices design. We will cite these concepts in the next chapters in an analog manner in order to simplify their understanding, although their complexity.

In this scenario, the monolith would symbolize a supermarket that encompasses a wide range of products such as apparel, groceries, and household cleaning items. In this case, if the grocery section has been impacted by any incident, electricity issues for example, and it was found that the issue fixing is going to take a whole day, in this case, the whole supermarket will be closed for a day, even in the face of customers who would want to buy something other than grocery products, which will induce large losses for the supermarket while waiting for the restoration of the impacted section (grocery). While in a shopping center, which will represent the analogy of microservices, the event of a significant incident at the shoe store, for example, will only affect the store itself and will be closed until the issue is resolved. However, customers of the shopping center will still be able to visit and make purchases from the other stores. This will minimize the financial loss of the shopping center and ensure customer satisfaction.

Skyward clouds:

Insights into main models

Cloud computing is the on-demand delivery of IT resources over the Internet with pay-as-you-go pricing. Instead of buying, owning, and maintaining physical data centers and servers, you can access technology services, such as computing power, storage, and databases, on an as-needed basis from a cloud provider like Amazon Web Services (AWS).

Amazon

It is widely recognized that there are three primary types of cloud computing: Software as a Service (SaaS), Platform as a Service (PaaS), and Infrastructure as a Service (IaaS). For commercial reasons, we don't mention the fourth primary type

17

which is the On-Premise as well. So, in this chapter, and so on, we will dive into real-world insights inspired by shopping centers.

Each type of cloud computing: SaaS, PaaS, IaaS or On-Premise, provides different levels of control, flexibility, and management so that you can select the right set of services for your needs.

$$***$$

1. Infrastructure as a Service (IaaS)

With IaaS, you rent the base infrastructure (space, servers, storage), and you are in charge of managing and maintaining everything above. In a similar vein, you are in charge of setting up and running your own store in a vacant commercial location.

The IaaS is similar to renting a vacant commercial space in a shopping center. You are in charge of building your store, equipping it up with shelves, escalators, and other types of gadgets, as well as managing public utilities like water and electricity.

18

2. Platform as a Service (PaaS)

PaaS provides you with a platform that is preconfigured, allowing you to develop and launch apps without having to worry about maintaining the underlying infrastructure. This is comparable to leasing office space  where everything you need is ready, freeing you up to concentrate on branding and growing your company.

PaaS is similar to leasing a business space that already comes equipped with fundamental furnishings like shelves and cash registers within a shopping center. All you need to do is customize the store's interior, which includes setting up the merchandise on the shelves and decorating the space.

3. Software as a Service (SaaS)

SaaS allows you to use a program that is hosted and maintained by a different company. Everything is supported for you, so you don't need to worry about infrastructure, upkeep, or software updates. It's similar to renting a completely furnished business location from which you may operate right away. SaaS is similar to leasing a fully furnished office space in a shopping center, complete with payment processors, salespeople, and even interior design. All you need to do is begin serving your customers with your own products.

4. On-Premise

On-premises computing allows you to administer and have complete control over all software and hardware on your own premises. Although you have total control, doing so comes with

additional costs and maintenance and upgrade duties. This is comparable to having complete control and accountability for your area when you own your business building in a mall.

Owning an on-premise space makes you totally responsible for the structure, design, construction, equipment, etc. Much like when you own the mall grounds of your own business. Everything from building to exhibiting, including upkeep and security, is your responsibility. which means that the mall doesn't build your commercial store like others who purchased already built shops like the IaaS and PaaS paradigms.

That being said, what about the cloud providers? What rule would they play in the shopping mall analogy? That's what we'll discover in the next part of this chapter.

5. Cloud providers

Cloud service providers like AWS (Amazon Web Services), Microsoft Azure and Google Cloud Platform (GCP) might be compared to well-known construction firms that specialize in creating and overseeing cutting-edge, high-performing shopping centers.

Similar to how AWS, Azure and GCP provide a wide range of cloud services, from data hosting to advanced analytics processing, these construction companies offer a wide range of services, from architectural design to operational management.

Similar to how a reputable building company may give creative, bespoke solutions to fit the unique requirements of its clients, Azure and GCP can offer scalable, personalized cloud solutions for businesses of all kinds.

These cloud providers aim to build dependable and effective infrastructures while offering cutting-edge services to satisfy the shifting demands of the market by putting a strong emphasis on quality, innovation, and sustainability.

Building tools: The Spring way

 In the context of software development, frameworks like Spring Boot for Java or others could be contrasted with a set of modern building/construction tools and technologies used by architects and engineers to effectively design and build shopping center infrastructure (The application). Here's how we might explain it:

Spring is a development platform that makes it easier and faster to create Java applications by providing default configurations and integrating a wide range of popular tools and packages. In our analogy, Spring Boot would be similar to a set of tools for construction that helps with the design and construction of malls using cutting-edge technologies and modern techniques.

Here are several Spring Boot characteristics and how they relate to our context:

1. Autoconfiguration

Spring Boot provides intelligent self-configuration, which configures various parts of the application depending on found dependencies. This would be similar to a team of experienced architects who automatically optimize the mall's design based on the project's individual requirements.

2. Starter POMs

Spring Boot start-ups make dependency management easier by offering predefined dependencies for various sorts of applications. This is analogous to a construction company employing premade models to speed up the design and building of a mall.

3. Easy integration

Spring Boot integrates several standard technologies seamlessly, allowing developers to focus on feature creation rather than configuration. This integration facility would be akin to a construction company using standardized equipment and materials to assure compatibility and consistency in the mall building.

Spring is analogous to a building company that specializes in the effective design and development of Java applications utilizing the latest technologies and best practices. Spring simplifies the development process and provides strong tools, allowing developers to construct robust, scalable systems while increasing productivity.

Microservices navigating:

Four key principles unveiled

Nowadays, successful microservice applications follow Heroku's twelve-factor manifesto (https://12factor.net/) in order to flourish. This manifesto outlines key principles for crafting contemporary, scalable, and sustainable software-as-a-service applications, which hold significant relevance for microservices development.

It is crucial to make a concerted effort to achieve alignment with these ideals. In this chapter, we aim to distill this comprehensive list to its bare essentials, providing a solid foundation for launching a microservices project on a strong footing. Additional principles can be progressively integrated as our application evolves over time.

The barest required minimum of these principles in MOA

(Microservice-Oriented Architecture) are:

- ➤ Loose coupling
- ➤ Dynamically configurable
- ➤ Service discovery
- ➤ Monitoring

1. Loose coupling

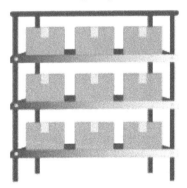

In order to guarantee the ability of a microservice to handle increasing demands and maintain a high level of dependability, it is essential to create it in a way that allows it to be deployed separately, while also enabling it to handle its own data and dependencies. This means each microservice should adhere to the single responsibility principle, focusing on a specific task or function. Interactions between microservices should be limited to task completion, promoting a modular and efficient system architecture. For further exploration of S.O.L.I.D principles, including the Single Responsibility Principle, delve into 'Main OOP SOLID Principles: A guide for curiously lazy yet smart learners' available on Amazon (Refer to the 91st page for more details!).

Getting back to the shopping center insight, well, every store operates as an autonomous unit, independent of the others and able to function as such. The remaining stores stay functioning properly if one is unexpectedly shut for whatever reason.

2. Dynamically configurable

In a typical scenario, a microservice is deployed across multiple environments, each necessitating its distinct configuration. Hardcoding the microservice configuration necessitates updating the application code in every environment, a cumbersome and impractical process.

33

The essence of this principle lies in decoupling the microservice configuration from the code. This separation enables seamless customization and deployment across diverse environments. By externalizing configuration, swift adjustments can be made without the need for code modifications, fostering agility and flexibility in deployment processes.

Imagine each store in a shopping mall as a microservice in your application ecosystem. A microservice should be adjustable in the same way that a store can tailor its services to its customer's desires. It should effortlessly update its product range to reflect market trends or change its working hours during busy seasons.

$$***$$

3. Service discovery

In a microservices environment, services are usually spread across multiple instances or containers, making it challenging for clients to find the appropriate service instances. The technique of dynamically finding and identifying accessible service instances

distributed context is known as service discovery.

It relies on a single source of truth, a centralized database known as the service registry, which maintains a global view of available service instances and their network locations. To locate the stores they want to head to, shoppers make use of interactive plan terminals situated throughout the mall. These terminals allow visitors to look at specific shops and provide an interactive map of the mall. In the unlikely circumstance that the shop has been closed temporarily or lacked the merchandise, the terminal would right away recommend nearby alternatives.

4. Monitoring

Microservices monitoring entails granular monitoring of individual and distributed services across boundaries, leveraging service discovery for dynamic monitoring, anomaly detection, proactive alerting, etc. It provides thorough observability into the performance, dependability, and behavior of distributed microservices architectures by using tools like Dynatrace, Prometheus, etc to gather and analyze metrics, traces, and logs.

All shops have an oversight mechanism established for keeping a watchful eye on the way things are progressing. As soon as a store encounters a glitch, such as a faulty cash register or an unforeseen incident, it immediately alerts the shopping center's main system to report the issue at hand. Visitors can keep shopping undisturbed through the interactive plan terminals, which get updated in real-time alongside this data and direct customers toward other stores.

Scaling the Heights:

The art of expansion & contraction

Scalability is a crucial aspect of microservices, particularly in modern applications that must manage changing loads efficiently. Scalability assures that an application can easily accommodate growth in terms of user base, data volume, or transaction rate without sacrificing performance.

Scalability in microservices is more than just handling more requests; it also means doing so efficiently and cost-effectively. It enables the dynamic allocation of resources to meet demand, whether by scaling up (adding more resources) during peak times or scaling down during off-peak hours to save money.

Furthermore, the distributed nature of microservices allows each service to be scaled individually, allowing granular control over resource use. This is especially critical for modern applications that may encounter unforeseen spurts of traffic and must maintain excellent performance and availability without overprovisioning resources.

Generally, we have two scaling types: the horizontal and the vertical. Horizontal scaling refers to adding new instances of a service to share the load, whereas vertical scaling includes adding resources (such as CPU or memory) to an already existing instance.

$$***$$

1. Horizontal scalability

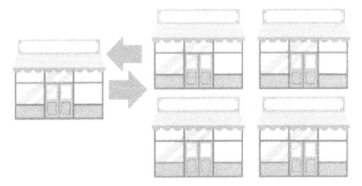

To illustrate the horizontal scalability aspect through our mall shopping experience. Let us assume that To accommodate increasing demand, horizontal scalability is adding equal or similar shops at several mall locations. It is comparable to a mall's horizontal expansion. To better serve clients, a mall may open many stores in various locations if a certain type of shop, like a clothing shop, is in high demand. By functioning autonomously and having the capacity to oversee its own clientele, every added store shares the workload and enhances the general customer experience.

Down Scalability: In contrast, the mall can modify its approach by closing some of its stores or concentrating its operations in one area if demand declines or becomes less consistent. For instance, in order to maximize expenses and resources, the mall may decide to eliminate some of the already added clothes stores or combine them with other businesses if they see a drop in foot traffic. The mall can respond to changes in the market with flexibility while maintaining operating efficiency thanks to this method.

2. Vertical scalability

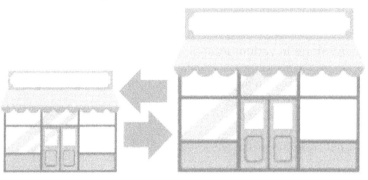

By comparison, vertical scalability refers to the process of enhancing and growing an already existing store in order to boost its capacity and overall performance, as opposed to the horizontal growth (duplication) of a single store. For instance, the mall might expand an existing clothes store by adding more floors or increasing its sales area rather than opening new ones. By enhancing its services and providing a wider range of products, this strategy helps the store provide better customer service while solidifying its identity and presence inside the mall.

The resilient microservice:

Beyond the break

Failures are like unwelcome visitors in the realm of systems: they appear unexpectedly, and it is up to the system's resilience to manage them gracefully. Failures in distributed systems, particularly in microservices-based architectures, can have catastrophic repercussions. Picture this: Service1 requires information from Service2, but Service2 is dependent on Service3, which is now offline. It's like a tangled web, where one blip triggers a cascade of difficulties, leaving the client stuck and unsure of what's going on.

To keep operations operating smoothly and consumers pleased, avoid such sticky situations. One wise decision is to create systems that detect errors as soon as they occur and respond quickly. But here's the tough bit. How can we figure out which service is acting up in a huge network of interconnected services?

This is where the true challenge lies. With so many moving pieces, it's like looking for a needle in a haystack. But no worries! There are tactics and instruments available to help us navigate these turbulent waters. There are solutions to this conundrum, ranging from strong monitoring systems that keep an eye on service health to sophisticated error-handling methods that reveal where things went wrong.

By investing in preventative steps and remaining watchful, we can ensure that our systems remain robust and our clients are satisfied even when breakdowns occur.

Consider resilience as a mall's capacity to bear and bounce back from unforeseen difficulties or interruptions while continuing to offer customers a secure and useful environment. Resilience is the capacity to take pre-emptive steps and be flexible in order to maintain stability in the face of difficulty, much like a mall that has backup power generators, security cameras, and fire alarms in place in case of an emergency. In general, the following important precautions should be taken:

1. Solid Infrastructure: The infrastructure and foundation of a resilient mall are strong. This entails sturdy support beams, well-constructed buildings, and dependable utility systems. Similar to this, having a strong foundation in life may help you weather unforeseen setbacks. This foundation can be anything from a robust support system to wholesome habits or stable finances.

2. Diverse Tenant Mix: To cater to a range of consumer tastes and financial situations, a prosperous mall diversifies its tenant base. In a similar vein, building diverse networks of support, interests, and abilities is essential to personal resilience. This guarantees that you won't be unduly dependent on one area of your life for stability, which will facilitate your capacity to adjust when things change.

3. Emergency Preparedness: Plans for dealing with a variety of emergencies, including fires, natural catastrophes, and security concerns, are in place for resilient malls. Similarly, being resilient entails having backup plans and coping mechanisms for any difficulties life may present. Being organized can make navigating difficult times easier, whether it's with regard to creating great relationships, managing your finances, or keeping your physical and emotional health in check.

4. Adaptability and Innovation: Malls that are innovative and adaptable survive shifting consumer preferences and macroeconomic environments. Similarly, being flexible and receptive to change are components of personal resilience. It entails having the flexibility to pick up new abilities, change course as needed, and come up with original solutions to issues.

Client-side resiliency patterns

Technically speaking, various resiliency patterns have evolved as best practices for dealing with failures in microservices. Each pattern handles distinct challenges, ensures the application's functionality, and acts consistently in the face of unexpected events. Developers can mix and combine these patterns to create a resiliency approach that is tailored to their application's specific requirements. Some of the most common client-side resiliency patterns are:

- ➢ Client-Side Load Balancing
- ➢ Circuit Breaker

> ➤ Bulkhead

> ➤ Fallback

By allowing the client to fail quickly and preventing the use of expensive resources like thread pools and database connections, these patterns hope to stop the problem with the distant service from propagating upstream to the client's consumers.

✳✳✳

1. Client-side load balancing pattern

In a client-side load balancing pattern, the physical location of each service instance is cached after the client queries a service discovery agent for each service's individual instances.

The client-side balancer can tell whether a service instance is acting strangely or throwing errors since it is positioned in between the service client and the service consumer. In this manner, in the case that the load-balancer discovers an issue, it can eliminate the impacted service instance from the pool of accessible service locations and stop that service instance from receiving any more service requests.

In a resilient microservices architecture, client-side load balancing is comparable to having interactive terminals strategically placed throughout the mall, providing real-time updates on store availability and directing customers to alternative locations. Imagine a large mall where some popular brands have multiple stores situated in different areas—north, east, west, and south. Each store represents a microservice within our analogy. The interactive terminals act as the "front planners," dynamically updating and guiding customers based on the current status of each store. If a store in the north section encounters issues and cannot serve customers, the interactive terminals inform incoming customers from the north entrance to visit stores in the east, west, or south sections instead. This resilience strategy optimizes customer experience by redistributing traffic to available stores, ensuring smooth operations and preventing overload in any single location.

✳✳✳

2. Circuit Breaker

When a remote service is called, the client resiliency pattern circuit breaker will keep an eye on the call. The circuit breaker will intervene and end the call if it goes on for too long. Whatever the design, it is directly derived from and fashioned after an electrical circuit breaker, which trips when it senses that too much current is passing through the line.

Additionally, the circuit breaker keeps track of every call made to a remote resource. If a sufficient number of these calls are unsuccessful, the circuit breaker implementation will trip, failing quickly and stopping further calls to the failing remote resource.

Breaker resilience in microservices is similar to having an emergency squad stationed around the mall. Each store has its own emergency response team that oversees its operations. If a store experiences a surge in traffic or encounters a problem with its cash register, for example, the emergency team will intervene to temporarily divert traffic away from the affected store if the involved brand has another store within the same mall, or simply stop the flow of customers within the store until the issues are resolved or the number of customers within the store is reduced, allowing new customers to be served on time. This proactive strategy reduces the impact of failures, maintains overall system stability, and assures uninterrupted service for clients, so their satisfaction is ensured.

3. Bulkhead

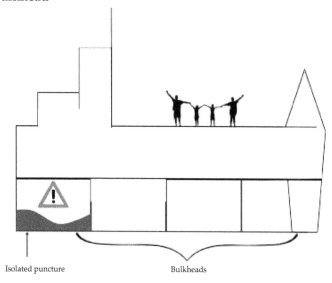

Isolated puncture   Bulkheads

The bulkhead design is derived from a shipbuilding notion. A ship with a bulkhead design is separated into entirely contained, segregated compartments known as bulkheads, even in the case that the hull is damaged, the water will be contained to the section of the ship where the puncture occurred, preventing the entire ship from filling with water and sinking.

A service that has to communicate with several remote resources can use the same idea. You can lower the chance that an issue with a single sluggish remote resource request would bring down the entire application by utilizing the bulkhead pattern to divide calls to distant resources into separate thread pools. Your service's bulkheads are the thread pools. Every distant resource is divided up and put into a thread pool. The thread pool for that particular type of service call will fill up and cease processing requests if one service is responding slowly. Because service calls are allocated to different thread pools, they won't become saturated.

Microservices' bulkhead resilience is analogous to a mall's stores being divided to contain problems and keep them from spreading to other sections. With well-defined borders and resources, each store runs autonomously within its own area, handling customer care service, promotions service, delivery service, etc. When a particular service fails—for example, due to overcrowding or exhaustion—it stays isolated and doesn't affect other services. For example, the delivery team can continue to operate regularly even if the customer service staff is overworked. This compartmentalization improves fault tolerance and guarantees the overall system's resilience.

4. Fallback

 When a remote service call fails, the service consumer will attempt to complete an action using an alternative code path and fallback pattern instead of raising an exception. This usually involves queuing the user's request for processing at a later time or searching for data from an additional data source. The user may be informed that their request will need to be performed at a later time, but their call will not display an exception indicating a problem.

Fallback processing resilience is akin to having backup stores in a mall to accommodate overcrowding or sudden closures. Each business identifies backup establishments that provide similar products or services to mall customers and can temporarily take over operations in the event of an interruption or overload. If a store encounters problems, such as technical failures or resource limits, traffic is smoothly routed to approved backup stores, ensuring service continuity. This resilience technique reduces disruptions and ensures service availability, even in difficult

circumstances.

Communicating in Microservices:

The Essential Guide

The design, development, and deployment of contemporary software systems have been completely transformed by microservices architecture. This architectural style's fundamental idea is to divide large, complicated applications into smaller, independently deployable services that combine to create a coherent whole. The real strength of microservices, however, is found not only in their individual capacities but also in their capacity for efficient cooperation and communication.

The core of a microservices architecture is communication. It is the mechanism that enables data sharing, action coordination, and system-wide event response amongst various dispersed components. Even the best-designed microservices would function in isolation and be unable to realize the full potential of this architectural approach in the absence of strong and effective

communication patterns.

Two main forms of communication have emerged as essential

components in the world of microservices: synchronous and

asynchronous communication. These patterns show various

methods of approaching service engagement, each with unique

traits, benefits, and difficulties.

$$***$$

1. Synchronous communication

Let's assume the shoppers are going straight to the various retail stores of the shopping center to make their purchases. When a buyer is willing to acquire an

item, they head straight towards the relevant store and make their

purchase.

This model enables direct and immediate communication. Before going to the next step, the customer makes a request (purchase) and then waits for a response (product acquisition). This is comparable to synchronous HTTP communication, in which, a client makes a request towards a specific microservice and keeps waiting for the response.

2. Asynchronous communication

When a customer searches for a specific product or wishes to get informed about discounts, the act of communicating his request and doing something about it is what we'll call an event. This could involve scanning a QR code to learn more about a product or subscribing to a newsletter to obtain exclusive deals. As soon as a customer initiates an event, such as a product request or a newsletter subscription, the retail outlet might respond favorably by ordering the missing coveted product, or by providing the requested data or serving new discounts.

In this model, customers create events according to their own requirements or wishes. Asynchronously responding to these events, concerned microservices (stores) offer the solutions or services shoppers have requested.

So in the asynchronous event communication paradigm, events are created by users (clients) and micro-services (stores) react to these events asynchronously by processing them appropriately.

The Data Warehouse:

Managing Databases in Microservices

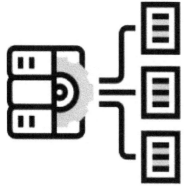 One fundamental principle of microservices is that each service handles its own data. Two services should not share the same data storage. Instead, each service is responsible for maintaining its own private data store, which other services do not have direct access to.

The purpose of this rule is to prevent inadvertent coupling between services, which might occur if services share the same underlying data model. If the data schema changes, it must be coordinated with all services that rely on that database. By separating each service's data store, we can limit the extent of change while maintaining the agility of completely independent deployments. Another reason is that each microservice may have unique data models, queries, and read/write patterns. Using a shared database Using a shared data store restricts each team's ability to optimize data storage for its own service.

Databases can be thought of as the respective storage regions of each microservice, acting as the persistent layer that maintains the service's state and data integrity

Let's assume that each store in a shopping mall represents a microservice or an API. Now, consider a scenario in which each merchant has a separate chamber dedicated solely to housing its items. For example, a clothing store would have a room to keep garments, but a shoe store would have a room to store shoes. This storage compartment functions as a database for the store, storing all of its contents.

Then there's a computer software that helps each retailer manage its inventory. This software allows employees to rapidly verify if a product is still in stock and where it is in the retail storage.

Then there's computer system, similar to software, that helps each retailer manage its inventory. Employees can use this software to rapidly determine whether a product is still in stock and where it is in retail storage area. It's similar to how cashiers could consult a catalog to determine whether a product is available for purchase and where to find it in the store.

As a result, each store operates independently with its own storage space and computer system to control its inventory, much as each microservice or API has its own database and software to manage its data. This ensures that information is organized and only available to authorized individuals, resulting in efficient and secure operation of each component.

Behind the Scenes:

Ensuring Visibility in Microservices

Software architectures must have Logs in order to assist record and monitoring actions. Multiple independent services that communicate with one another make up a microservice architecture. Accurate problem diagnosis and understanding of system behavior across services depend on logging.

One way to follow application requests as they go from front-end devices to databases and back-end services is through distributed tracing. Distributed tracing can be used by developers to troubleshoot queries that show faults or significant latency.

An application is divided into modular services using

71

microservice architecture. Each service manages a key application function and is frequently overseen by a specialized team.

Because microservices sometimes operate on complex, distributed backends and because queries may consist of a series of many service calls, troubleshooting them can be difficult. By utilizing distributed end-to-end tracing.

When a user fills out a form on a website, for example, end-to-end distributed tracing platforms start gathering data right away. This causes the tracing platform to create an initial span known as the parent span and a unique trace ID. A trace is a representation of the request's whole execution route, with each span in the trace denoting a distinct task completed along the way, such as an API call or database query. A top-level child span is formed whenever the request enters a service.

If the request contained several commands or inquiries within the same service, the child span at the top level might serve as a parent-to-child span underneath it. Each child span is encoded by the distributed tracing platform with the original trace ID, a distinct span ID, duration and error data, and pertinent metadata, like the customer ID or location.

72

***

Distributed Tracing vs. Logging

Distributed tracing and logging enable developers to monitor and troubleshoot performance issues. Logs might come from the application, infrastructure, or network layers, and each time-stamped log highlights a specific event in your system. When a container runs out of memory, it may send out a log message. A distributed trace, on the other hand, occurs exclusively at the application layer and offers information about a request as it moves across service borders. A trace allows you to see the complete request flow and pinpoint the location of any bottlenecks or errors that occurred. Examining the logs linked with the request may help you go deeper into the core cause of the slowness or issue.

In our mall analogy, the security and surveillance staff would serve as an excellent illustration.

Consider that the mall's security and surveillance team has installed security cameras and an alarm system to protect merchants and customers while also monitoring activities across the entire structure.

1. Logging

Surveillance cameras continuously record mall happenings and activity, just as computer logging does. These records allow transactions, acquaintances, and occurrences to be documented for later examination.

2. Monitoring

Surveillance cameras are linked to a centralized monitoring system, which analyzes video streams in real-time to detect suspicious activity or abnormal situations.

Similarly, IT monitoring solutions like Splunk or Dynatrace scan logs and metrics from applications and infrastructures to detect anomalies, errors, or poor performance.

3. Alert Notification

When the video surveillance system identifies suspicious activity, it sends an alarm to the security personnel, who investigate and respond appropriately. Similarly, when an IT monitoring system finds unexpected occurrences or defects in logs, it notifies operational personnel. These signals allow teams to respond quickly to problems, reducing downtime and improving system reliability.

Lock and Key:

Securing Microservices with OAuth 2.0

A mechanism known as OAuth 2.0, or "Open Authorization,"
allows a website or application to access resources hosted by other
web apps on the user's behalf. OAuth 2.0 allows for consented
access to resources while never disclosing the user's credentials.

OAuth2.0 guiding principles

OAuth 2.0 is a permission mechanism, not an authentication
protocol. As a result, its primary goal is to enable access to a
variety of resources, such as user data or remote APIs.

We use Access Tokens with OAuth 2.0. An access token is a piece
of information that represents the end-user's permission to access
resources. OAuth 2.0 does not specify an Access Token's format.
Nonetheless, the JSON Web Token (JWT) format is commonly used

in certain scenarios. This allows token issuers to embed data within the token. Additionally, Access Tokens may have an expiration date for security concerns.

OAuth 2.0 Roles

Roles are an essential component of the OAuth2.0 authorization framework standard. These identify the following as the fundamental components of an OAuth 2.0 system:

o **Resource Owner**: The person or entity that owns the protected resources and has the authority to authorize access.

o **Client**: refers to the system that requires access to protected resources. To access resources, the client must have the correct Access Token.

o **Authorization Server**: This server processes access token requests from the Client following a successful authentication process and approval from the Resource Owner. The authorization server provides two endpoints: the token endpoint, which is used for machine-to-machine communication, and the authorization endpoint, which handles user consent and interactive authentication.

o **Resource server**: a server that grants access requests from the client while protecting the users' resources. It returns the required resources to the client after accepting and verifying the Access Token.

OAuth 2.0 scopes

Scopes are an important feature of OAuth 2.0. They serve to clarify why someone may be granted access to resources. The Resource Server determines both allowable scope values and the resources to which they apply.

***

Authorization Code and OAuth 2.0 Access Token

Following the Resource Owner's authorization for access, the OAuth 2 Authorization server may not immediately return an Access Token. An Authorization Code might be returned instead, which would give more security. It is then exchanged for an access token. In addition to the Access Token, the Authorization server may issue a Refresh Token. Refresh Tokens, unlike Access Tokens, often have longer expiration periods and can be redeemed for new Access Tokens at that point. Clients must store Refresh Tokens safely owing to their unique qualities.

Now with this being said, here comes the best part of the book. Let's use our mall shopping journey to simplify the OAuth concept. But prior to delving into the OAuth process, let us go over the previous details and offer an analogy for each of them:

o **Resource Owner:** The customer who enters the mall and carries sensitive information on his bank card.

o **Client**: To handle customer transactions, the store employs an electronic payment terminal (EPT). To finish the transaction, the entity requesting the buyer's private bank card details is the EPT.

o **Authorization Server**: The bank's security system. The buyer's bank card information cannot be accessed by the EPT unless the bank's security systems grant permission.

o **Resource server**: Represents the bank that holds the buyer's credit card information. This is where sensitive data is stored and protected. In simple words, the customer's bank!

Here is a scenario of what happens:

1. Request for Bank Card Information

The buyer's bank card information is requested by the EPT (client application) from the bank's security system (the authorization server). This request includes, among other things, the scope of the requested information, the client's name (EPT), and the redirect URL to which the results will be sent.

2. Authorization Server Response

The bank's security system (authorization server) reviews the application and, if agreed upon, generates a private and public key pair for the EPT. He then transmits the public key to the EPT together with an authorization code (if following the Authorization Code Grant flow) or directly issues a token (if using the Client Credentials Grant flow).

✳✳✳

3. Signing the Access Token

The EPT receives an access token from the bank's security system (the authorization server). Then using the private key, it (the EPT) signs the received access token (JWT) with the requested information and transmits it to the bank (resource server) for verification.

4. Verification by the Bank

The bank confirms the JWT's signature as proof of validity by comparing it with the already generated private key (in the second step of this flow).

5. Processing the Transaction

If the signature is valid, the bank will extract the bank card information from the JWT buyer and use it to process the transaction.

This illustration shows how OAuth 2.0 enables a third-party application (EPT) to get sensitive information from a resource owner (the buyer) after receiving authorization from the authorization server (the bank), and how the information is then securely used to complete a transaction.

Conclusion

In recent years, microservices have become more popular. However, this in no way suggests that they are the ideal architecture to use at any cost. On the other hand, perspective is always required when it comes to the architectural selection of its application based on several factors, including the likelihood that one component will undergo a more substantial evolution than the others, the frequency of updates, and the number of possible users.

Not to mention that we always have access to well-known, somewhat monolithic programs on hand these days, such as Microsoft Word. If each architecture fits the requirements and development goals of the intended application, it would be the best option.

Thank you

I hope you enjoyed reading "Come Shop with Me: Discovering Microservices, One Store at a Time." I also hope you enjoyed the analogical and metaphorical writing style I crafted; it took a lot of thought to establish. I'm grateful that you finished the book and made it thus far.

Your support is very appreciated, and I hope the insights and analogies have helped you better grasp microservices. Thank you for joining me on this adventure; I look forward to hearing your opinions!

Discover More with My Previous Book!

MASTERING

OOP | SOLID

PRINCIPLES

A Guide For Curiously Lazy Yet Smart
Learners through real-world insights

ATIF **A.EDEN**

Discover "Mastering OOP / SOLID Principles: A Guide For Curiously Lazy Yet Smart Learners Through Real-World Insights." This concise guide breaks down nine key OOP principles, including Abstraction, Encapsulation, Inheritance, Polymorphism, and the S.O.L.I.D principles, using clear, real-world examples.

Perfect for seasoned developers, juniors, or curious learners, this book delivers substance without technical jargon. It's language-independent, focusing on conceptual aspects applicable to Python, Java, C#, and more.

Elevate your programming skills with this practical, accessible resource to enhance your programming knowledge?

Grab your copy of "Mastering OOP SOLID Principles" today!

Take notes here

www.ingramcontent.com/pod-product-compliance
Lightning Source LLC
Chambersburg PA
CBHW070837070326
40690CB00009B/1584